EARTH

Lynn M. Stone

Rourke
Publishing LLC
Vero Beach, Florida 32964

www.rourkepublishing.com

PHOTO CREDITS: Title Page: © NASA; page 4: © Daniela Andreea Spyropoulos; page 5: © NASA; pages 6-7: © Dan Wood; page 8: © sonyae; page 9: © Alexander Hafemann, ilker canikligil; page 10: © Tammy Peluso; page 11: © Nina Shannon; pages 12-13: © Dan Wood; pages 14-15: © René Mansi; pages 16-17: © NASA; pages 18-19: © GEORGE TOUBALIS; page 20: © Ufuk ZIVANA; page 22: © NASA

Editor: Meg Greve

Cover and Interior designed by: Tara Raymo

Library of Congress Cataloging-in-Publication Data

Stone, Lynn M.
  Earth / Lynn Stone.
     p. cm. -- (Skywatch)
  Includes index.
  ISBN 978-1-60472-293-2
  1. Earth--Juvenile literature. I. Title.
  QB631.4.S763 2009
  525--dc22
                                      2008024848

Printed in the USA

CG/CG

Table of Contents

The Earth 4

Life on Earth 8

The Earth's Moon 12

The Earth in the Solar System 16

Glossary 23

Index 24

The Earth

The Earth is the **planet** on which we live.
It is the third closest planet to our Sun.

The Earth is believed
to be about 4.5 billion years old,
which is young compared to other
objects in space!

The Earth is shaped like a ball, although it is not an exact sphere. It **orbits** around the Sun in a nearly perfect circular path.

91.5 Million Miles to

As it orbits, the Earth stays between 91.5 million miles (147 million kilometers) and 94.5 million miles (152 million kilometers) away from the Sun. This orbit is what causes seasons to change on most parts of the Earth.

94.5 Million Miles

Life on Earth

Earth is the only planet that supports life as we know it.

Some places on Earth can be extremely hot or cold. Most life on Earth exists where temperatures are not too extreme.

9

Earth also has lots of water and the air we need to breathe. Air is what makes up the Earth's **atmosphere**.

Water and air support all life on Earth, such as plants, animals, and humans.

11

The Earth's Moon

Earth has one moon, which is about 240,000 miles (384,000 kilometers) away.

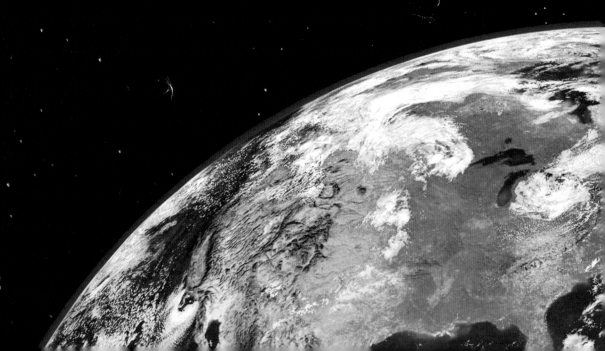

The force of Earth's gravity holds the Moon in orbit.

240,000 miles

The Moon's gravity is not as strong as the Earth's gravity. However, with the help of the Sun, the Moon's gravity controls the ocean's **tides**.

Low Tide

14

In most places there are two high tides and two low tides each day.

High Tide

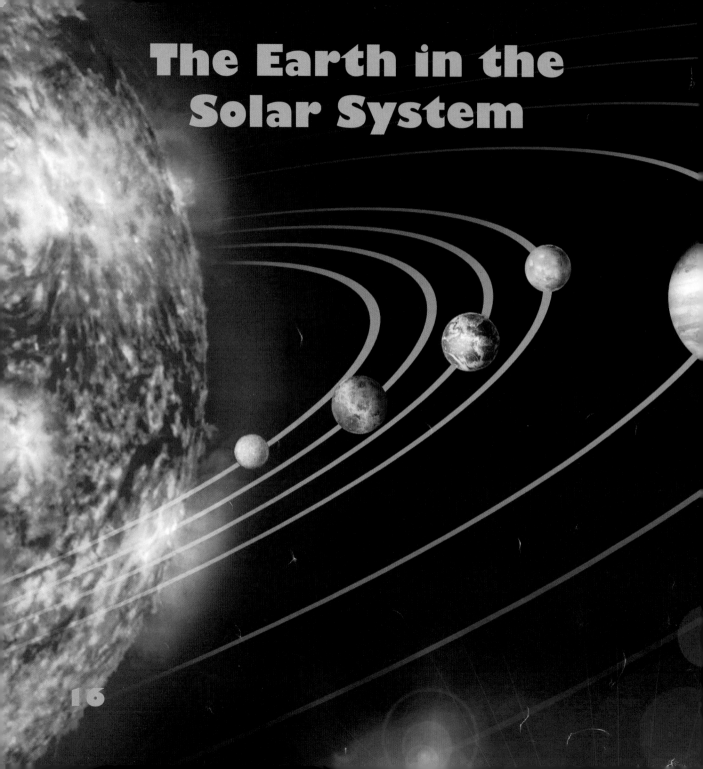

The Earth in the Solar System

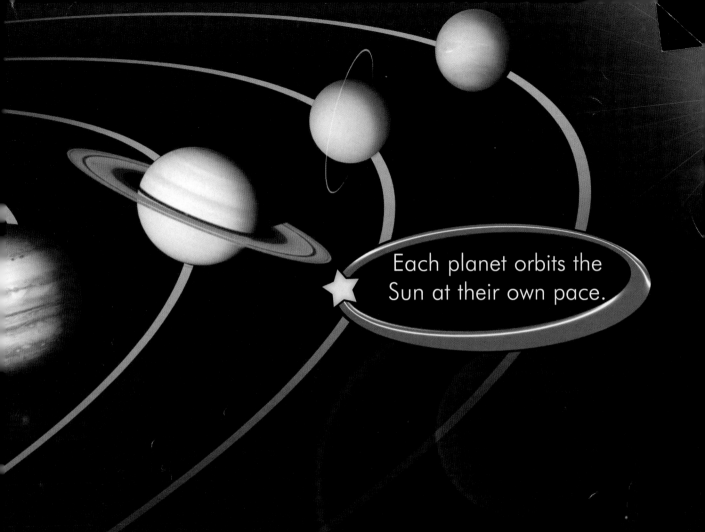

Each planet orbits the Sun at their own pace.

The Earth is one of eight planets in our **solar system**. One orbit around the Sun takes Earth about 365 days, or one year.

An imaginary line around the Earth's middle, known as the **equator**, measures 24,902 miles (40, 075 kilometers). That makes Earth the largest of the four inner planets.

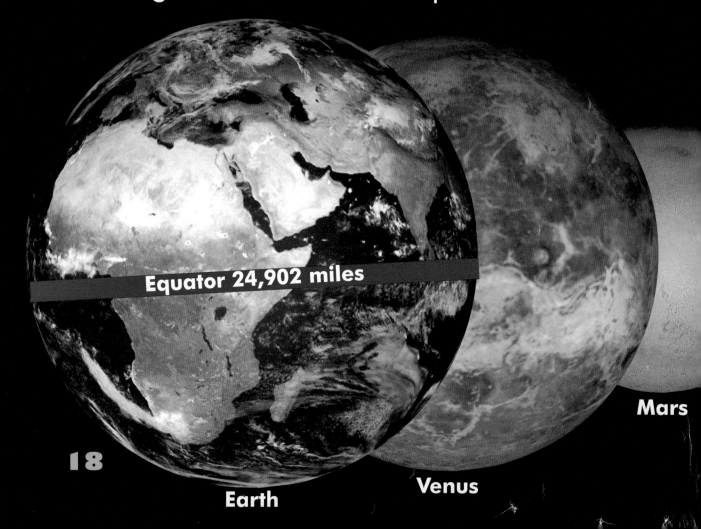

Equator 24,902 miles

Mars

Venus

Earth

The largest of the four outer planets is Jupiter.

Jupiter 88,846 miles

Mercury

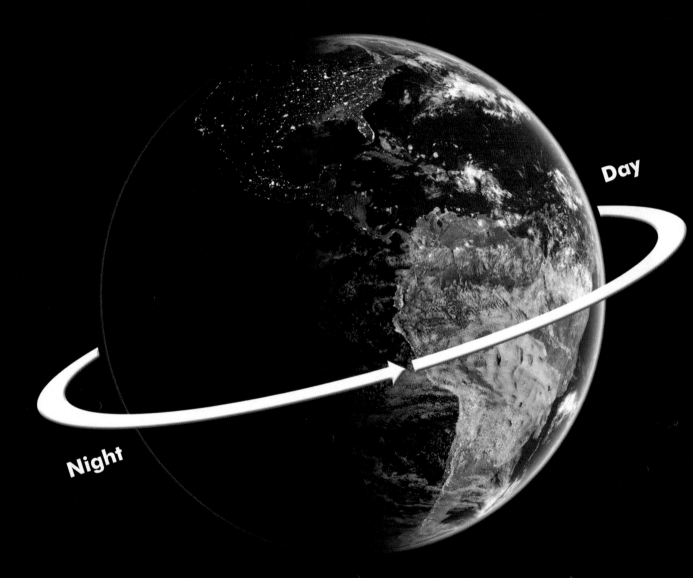

Day

Night

On Earth, the Sun appears from the east and sets in the west.

The Earth also spins while orbiting the Sun. The spin tilts part of the Earth toward the Sun. Because of the spinning motion, each part of the Earth takes a turn with daylight and darkness.

Even though we explore the Earth every day, space exploration continues as we try to discover new worlds and learn more about our own, the Earth.

An astronaut with a jetpack flies free of his spacecraft above the Earth.

Glossary

atmosphere (AT-muhs-fihr): a mixture of gases that surrounds a planet

equator (i-KWAY-tur): the distance around the Earth at its middle point between the poles

orbits (OR-bits): circular paths that an object in space follows around another object in space, such as the moon orbiting the Earth

planet (PLAN-it): any one of the several huge, ball-shaped objects in outer space that travels around the Sun

solar system (SOH-lur SISS-tuhm): the Sun and those objects in space bound to it by gravity

tides (TIDES): the rise and fall of the Earth's oceans caused by the pull of gravity from the Sun and Moon

Index

air   10, 11
atmosphere   10
daylight   19
equator   18
orbit   6, 7, 13, 17

seasons   7
Sun   4, 6, 11, 17, 21
tides   14
water   10, 11

Further Reading

Aquilar, David. 11 *Planets: A New View of the Solar System*. National Geographic, 2008.

Kerrod, Robin. *Planet Earth*. Lerner, 2003.

Twist, Clint. *The Earth*. School Specialty Publishing, 2006.

Websites to Visit

www.discoverspace.org
kids.earth.nasa.gov
http://solarsystem.nasa.gov/kids/index.cfm

About the Author

Lynn M. Stone is a widely-published wildlife and domestic animal photographer and the author of more than 500 children's books. His book *Box Turtles* was chosen as an Outstanding Science Trade Book and Selectors' Choice for 2008 by the Science Committee of the National Science Teachers' Association and the Children's Book Council.

24